The URBAN AMERICA SERIES is concerned with the most important and most alarming problems which face our cities today. From the ghettos, from colleges, universities, consulting services and research centers, the authors have brought to students dramatic evidence of many of our cities' social illnesses in a clear and direct manner, in an attempt to show what is wrong and what there is to do about it.

OTHER TITLES AVAILABLE IN THIS SERIES

VENEREAL DISEASE

ELIZABETH S. WILLIAMS

ALAN J. BURNES, ED.D., EDITOR

URBAN AMERICA SERIES

PENDULUM PRESS, INC.
BROOKS CORNER
WESTPORT, CONNECTICUT 06880

Published by

PENDULUM PRESS, INC.
BROOKS CORNER
WESTPORT, CONNECTICUT 06880

VENEREAL DISEASE brings the study and observation of this age-old problem into a sharp perspective, so that it can be viewed as it concerns teen-agers and young adults in the fast-paced world of today. In accenting the personal and emotional problems involved, the author uses case studies which illustrate that experience and understanding, not social status, determines the risk of infection. The "workings" of such diseases, particularly syphilis and gonorrhea, are presented in parallel languages which, though technically precise, are common to the discussions among young people.

TABLE OF CONTENTS

Back in olden times—you know, when your Mom and Dad were making the high school scene—that might make it before World War II, a bit—the really hip people talked about a lot of things by initials. There was the OPA, WPA, NRA, all government agencies, the boss was J.B., your grandfather was the O.M. (old man, of course!) and VD was that SOMETHING that everybody knew, but whispered about.

To be sure, it ranked with S-E-X, in the order of unspeakable-abouts. The swingers of that dim, dark day nodded wisely when those initials came up in conversation, and everybody assumed that OF COURSE you knew what the initials stood for, and what it was all about. And, like a lot of other things, that it wasn't "nice" to talk about. Very few questions were raised, and very few people—guys or gals—really knew that VD stood for Venereal Disease.

If your Dad had asked his father to clue him, very likely your grandfather would have asked, with some concern, "Where did you ever hear about THAT? Have you been hanging around with that crowd from downtown again?

Don't let me hear you mention that again—especially in front of your mother or your sister. 'Nice' (there it is again!) people don't talk about things like that!"

Well, there's the picture. So how DID your O.M. get the word? It shouldn't come as too much of a surprise to find out that, even in those days, the grapevine was operating pretty much the same as it does today. And if one guy got one piece of information and another a bit more, it didn't take long for communication systems to put it all together. Did you ever play that game, when one person whispers a sentence to the one next to him, and he passes it down, and so on, until finally the guy at the end says out loud and clear what it was that he heard. Boy! Is it ever different. Funny thing, but that may be JUST the way a lot of what we call Old Wives Tales about venereal disease got started.

Throughout history, information—or, the word—gets passed one way or another from generation to generation. If it's something "nice" people DO talk about, the information is usually right in line. But if it's the sort of thing that's whispered about, the facts become distorted—just as in the game—and a lot of MIS-information gets handed down. And because a lot of folks felt the way your grandparents did, most kids believed the stuff that got passed around the grapevine route.

What are some of those bits and pieces of mis-information that got handed down? Some of them will have a familiar ring to you. ("I *did* hear *that*. You mean it isn't true?")

You can get VD from public toilets, and that's why you were told never to sit on them.

If you touch a doorknob that someone who had it touched—there you are! Or cups, forks, spoons, etc.

Lifting things that are too heavy—especially for guys—can give it to you.

On that note, go ahead and run off to your next class, a little late. If you don't have to leave this class yet, and are as uncertain about the causes, symptoms and treatments of venereal disease as the other kids were, stick with us, and we'll try to answer your questions.

"Kill you?" said a couple of girls.

"Yeah, kill you, blind you, make you insane, make you sterile, so you can't have any kids; syph can do them all," said Dave.

"Hey, what happens to you if you get these things? How do you get rid of them? You wash a lot or something?"

"I don't think they have a vaccine for it yet."

"Yeah, I guess you just wait around to see if you go blind or crazy."

"Sometimes you can persuade a doctor to give you a special cure. Even if you're cured though, you can't have normal sex relations for years, and you have to have weekly examinations for a long time too. My mother told me that when she was warning me against VD."

"If you do get cured, you can't get it again, though, I bet. You become immune."

"Oh, that's a lot of bull. You can get cured, and then have more sex, and get it again. Just last night my brother told me a friend of his had clap for the third time. It revolts me, but the guy goes and gets some shot and then doesn't worry much more about it."

"I can't believe all these stories are true. I thought venereal disease went out back in the dark ages with the plague. So, we shouldn't have to worry about it."

PART III: WHY SHOULD YOU KNOW
MORE ABOUT VD?

Venereal disease is a serious and important disease in the United States. Its consequences are often tragic and permanent. If you contract the disease but don't know what you have and don't treat it, you suffer. Untreated, both syphilis and gonorrhea leave all their victims sterile or, in other words, unable to have babies.

Gonorrhea is a terrible disease. It can cause infected mothers to give birth to blind babies. As protection from the possibility, all babies receive special eyedrops at birth. Untreated gonorrhea may attack your heart, seriously disabling you. Or, it may afflict your joints, swelling them painfully.

The effects of uncured gonorrhea are bad, but the effects of uncured syphilis are even worse. Syphilis kills! Three thousand Americans a year die from syphilis. This is twenty times more than the number of Americans who die from such notorious diseases as the plague, typhoid, smallpox, and polio. Often, the person who contracts syphilis but doesn't treat it takes not only his own life, but another's as well. Infected mothers may give birth to dead babies. Or, if the baby isn't dead, chances are he will be syphilitic. Sometimes, he will be puny and deformed. Other times, he will be covered with nasty sores; he may be crippled, and there may be brain damage, or mental retardation. Syphilis affects adults in these same ways; it cripples victims, blinds them, and affects their mental processes.

Syphilis affects so many people in these ways that we spend $50 million a year to maintain victims of syphilitic insanity in mental hospitals, and another $6 million a year to care for the victims of syphilitic blindness.

Gonorrhea and syphilis are serious diseases not only because their consequences are grave when untreated, but also because the number of cases is very high here in the United States. Gonorrhea, the less dangerous disease, attacks a million Americans for the first time each year. Syphilis, the more dangerous disease, attacks about one hundred thousand. The less dangerous disease, gonorrhea, is ten times as common as syphilis. If we look at the incidence of venereal disease from another angle, the rate (the number of cases per number of people), we find its incidence is extremely high. Together, syphilis and gonorrhea infect about 10 million Americans over ten years time, or, one out of every 20 Americans. Rates are highest in cities, and the urban American has even greater chances of getting the disease.

VD rates are climbing. They have skyrocketed. Since 1961, rates of both syphilis and gonorrhea have tripled. In a few urban areas, VD is up 800%; in many others, it is up 500%. These rates of increase are unbelievably high and frightening.

Who's responsible for these soaring rates of VD? Often, teenagers. Every day, about 600 American teenagers like you are infected with VD. These days add up. Every year, about 200,000 teenagers are attacked by the disease. Teenagers account for about one of five cases of the disease, although they account for only one of every eight persons in the country. If we add people over 19 but under 25 to the teenagers, we find that these two sets of young people together account for one of every two cases of venereal disease, although they account for one of every four persons in the country. Further, the rates of venereal disease are spiralling upwards as fast or faster for these young people as they are for older people.

Why should all of us, especially the high school population, be increasingly concerned with the VD problem? Basically, more of you are experiencing sex before you marry, and sex with more than one partner, than ever before. Many of you experience sex today when you wouldn't have a few years ago, because of the availability of birth control pills and because of the spread of liberal attitudes toward premarital sex. Your experience creates many important moral issues; for example, you may experiment with sex for fun, but then be totally unprepared for the emotional results of the experiment. These moral issues are very complex and demand more consideration than we can give here.

On the other hand, sexual experience also creates health issues, and these are not as complex. In fact, the health issue is simple. If you experiment with sex, you must be prepared to accept VD as a possible consequence. You must know how serious the effects of VD can be, not only for yourself, but also for all those with whom you share intimate contact. You must know the symptoms of VD so that you can recognize it if you contact it, and then you must seek treatment for it, and PRONTO.

PART IV: TELLING IT LIKE IT IS:

GONORRHEA

Gonorrhea is the most common venereal disease. It accounts for 90 percent of the cases reported.

What causes gonorrhea? Like most venereal diseases, it's caused by germs transmitted through intimate sexual contact. You get gonorrhea through this contact, and only this contact. You *never* get it from dirty toilets, dirty dishes, or dirty doorknobs, as some high school students in our first chapter thought. You don't even get it from minor physical contact, such as shaking hands or kissing. You get it from sexual intercourse. The only exceptions to this rule are babies, who contract gonorrhea from the infected blood of their mother before they are born, and who may also contract it once in a great while merely from sleeping by the side of their infected mother, since their skin is so easily penetrated by infection.

You may be curious about the germ which transmits gonorrhea. This germ is called a gonococcus. Usually found in pairs, gonococci are spherically shaped and appear through a microscope like miniature coffee beans with their flat sides together. The gonococci germs must be carried wherever they go by body fluids. This is why you can't contract the disease from a toilet seat or from a wet dish. The germ can't live in a dry place or even in a damp place if the moisture isn't a body fluid. In body fluids, the gonococci enter another person through "mucous membrane," the soft, moist tissue of their sex organs.

How can you tell if the gonococci germs have entered your body? The symptoms which will tell you vary, depending on whether you are a man or a woman. In a man, the gonococci usually attack the mucuous membrane lining his urethra, the tube inside his penis through which urine and sperm pass out of his body. Generally, he doesn't realize this for the first couple of days after contracting the disease. Then, five days or so later, a thick whitish fluid, called pus, begins to drip slowly from his penis. By this time, his urethra is raw and sore, so that every time he urinates, or passes water, it hurts and burns. In review, we see that the two basic symptoms of gonorrhea in men are 1) a discharge of pus from the penis and 2) a painful burning sensation when passing water. These symptoms are always noticeable and painful enough so that infected men realize they need a doctor, and usually go to see one.

In a woman, the symptoms of gonorrhea are different; they are not as severe. The gonococci usually attack the mucuous membrane inside her vagina. Since the woman does not pass water through her vagina, she does not feel pain in urinating, as the male does. Also, because her vagina has other kinds of natural discharges and has a much larger area than the man's penis, she isn't as likely to notice the pus coming from this area as much as a man does from himself. Frequently, a woman does not detect any signs of gonorrhea at all. Yet, she is just as infectious as the diseased man. She can pass the disease along easily even though she doesn't know she has it. And, if she is pregnant, she can pass it on to her unborn baby.

In sum, because the symptoms of gonorrhea are slight in

a woman, she often waits until she has passed it on to someone else. Until he tells her she gave him the disease, she may not realize she has it and seek treatment for it. But, if there is the slightest question whether or not she might have gonorrhea, she should seek treatment to prevent infecting other people.

The only really noticeable symptom the woman experiences with gonorrhea often comes too late. This symptom is pain in her fallopian tubes, the tubes above her vagina where her ova or egg cells are fertilized by male sperm in the process of conception of babies. Usually, this pain signals that the gonococci have spread to her fallopian tubes and made her sterile (unable to have a baby). At this point, any woman knows she must seek a doctor, but he can only prevent the disease from damaging her further. He can't make her fertile again. If a man waits too long to find a doctor after the onset of gonorrhea, he will also experience some damage to his sex organs and may also become sterile.

So, when either a man or a woman suspects a gonorrhea infection, he or she should quickly go to a doctor or to the public health center and have the illness diagnosed. Then, if he discovers he's infected, he can warn his past sexual partners and can stop further sexual relations until he is cured. Unfortunately, diagnosis of gonorrhea is not always simple. There is no acceptable blood test for gonorrhea. A laboratory smear test, which examines discharged pus in an effort to detect gonococci, succeeds 99 times out of 100 in diagnosing gonorrhea in the male. But, this smear test unfortunately doesn't succeed with women. To diagnose gonorrhea in the female, doctors usually take a culture of their discharged pus. In other words, they try to see if they can grow the gonococci from the pus. If they succeed, the woman is infected.

After doctors discover that a person is infected by gonorrhea, they begin treatment. Today, treatment is relatively rapid and easy, as long as it is begun promptly. The sooner treatment is started, the more effective it is. It's important to realize though that only a doctor's treatment is effective. "Quack cures," such as salves and ointments and other common medicines bought in drugstores are completely ineffective. They don't work.

The drug most doctors use to treat gonorrhea is penicillin. Penicillin is not only highly effective, it is cheap and easy to administer. With men, two injections of penicillin are usually enough to cure gonorrhea. With women, more injections may be necessary. The length of treatment varies considerably. Although penicillin is the best weapon against gonorrhea, there are other drugs which are used with patients who are sensitive to penicillin, or who have built up an immunity to it. These include a whole host of new antibiotic drugs. Experiments are now in progress to determine the most effective methods of using these drugs in treating gonorrhea.

Treatment for gonorrhea also involves other procedures. First, patients should return to the health center two or three times for tests, to make sure their disease is completely cured. Secondly, patients should advise nurses of the names of all people with whom they have had sexual contact recently. But, more on these things later.

Is there any way you can make sure you won't get gonorrhea if you engage in sexual contact? No. There is no vaccine which immunizes you against the disease. There is no shot you can receive which protects you from it. Gonorrhea is not like polio, or typhoid, or tetanus. Shots don't protect you.

Nor does one infection with gonorrhea protect you from it in the future. You can contract it again, just as severely. You never build up immunity against it, even if you contract it ten times. But, though you don't build up immunity to gonorrhea, you may to penicillin. Repeated infection often makes it more and more difficult to treat. But, the infection generally doesn't become less severe after it's contracted two or three times.

We hope you now have a clear understanding of the causes, symptoms, and treatment of gonorrhea. Now, we'll turn to the second major American strain of venereal disease, a less common, but more dangerous strain: syphilis.

PART V: TELLING IT LIKE IT IS:

SYPHILIS

Syphilis kills! Although we have already observed that syphilis is lethal, let's run it by again. Untreated syphilis kills, cripples, blinds, and inflicts insanity. It tears at the skin. It digs holes in feet, knees, and faces. It is a dangerous and ugly disease.

Like gonorrhea, syphilis is contracted 99 times out of 100 from sexual intercourse, the one percent being reserved for entry through open sores or wounds. And, like gonorrhea, it's transmitted to babies through the blood of their mother if she is infected with syphilis during pregnancy. However, unlike gonorrhea, syphilis can also be contracted through skin-to-skin contact of any kind. Why can syphilis be transmitted in more and less intimate ways than gonorrhea?

The answer to this question lies in the nature of the syphilis germ, which is different from the gonorrhea germ. Syphilis is caused by a germ called a spirochete, a small germ shaped like a corkscrew. Like the gonococcus, which causes gonorrhea, the spirochete survives only in a moist warm environment such as the inside of the body, and usually enters other bodies through moist mucuous membranes in the genital organs. The spirochete has properties, however, that the gonococcus doesn't. First, it can grow in the mucuous membrane of the mouth as well as of the genitals, and so can be transmitted through kissing. Sec-

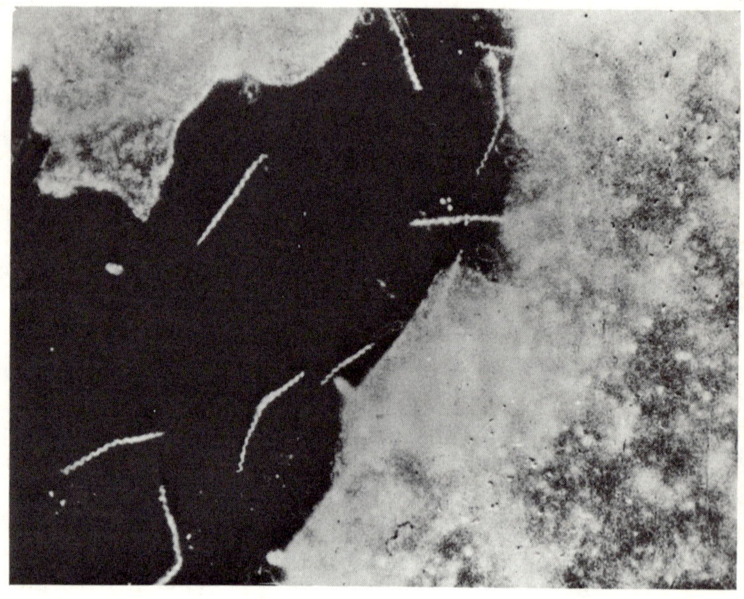

The tiny, corkscrew-like organism in this picture is the spirochete, or syphilis germs, as seen under special "dark-field" microscope. It's average length is only 3/10,000 of an inch, or approximately the diameter of a red blood cell.

ondly, it can enter any skin surface which is cut or broken. As a result, syphilis can be transmitted through any kind of skin-to-skin contact. Yet, the spirochete is a delicate, frail germ which dies quickly when it is exposed to soap and water, heat, dryness, light, and even air. Since it can't live outside the human body for more than seconds, it can't be transmitted through doorknobs, dishes, or toilet seats, just as gonorrhea can't.

How do you know if you have contracted syphilis? The symptoms of the disease are varied and generally occur in different phases. One symptom comes and then disappears, but its disappearance does not signal the end of the infection, unless the victim has been treated by a doctor. It merely means that the victim has passed into another phase of the disease.

After spirochetes enter the body, they pass into the blood and spread to other organs and tissues. The spirochetes multiply; in a few days, five billion worm-like germs are crawling inside the body. But, the victim doesn't feel any discomfort. He doesn't know he is sick. This initial, symptomless period of syphilis lasts anywhere from nine to ninety days, but averages about twenty days.

After these first few weeks, the disease enters its "primary phase." This phase is marked by the appearance of a small sore where the spirochete first entered the body. This small sore is called a "chancre" (shank'-er). Usually, it doesn't hurt. Sometimes, it's located high up inside the genital organs or in the back of the mouth, and so isn't even seen. Hopefully, the victim spots the chancre and gets treatment. If he doesn't, the chancre will disappear, but other symptoms will replace it.

From three to six weeks after the chancre emerges, the secondary stage of syphilis begins. The symptoms of this stage resemble the symptoms of many other diseases. Sometimes, the syphilis symptoms look like the common cold. The victim suffers from a sore throat, a headache, and a runny nose. He may lose weight. The lymph nodes may become enlarged. Hair may fall out. Or, the symptoms may resemble the measles. A rash may appear on the palms of the hands and on the soles of the feet. Sometimes, it covers the whole body.

Finally, ugly sores or lesions develop, frequently on the genitals and the mouth. These rashes and sores may be loaded with spirochetes, all highly infectious to anyone who touches them. Any and all of these symptoms may disappear and then come back, after a month or, perhaps, after twelve months for a period of up to two years. As with the chancre, the disappearance of these symptoms never signals the cure of syphilis unless the victim has been treated by a doctor.

After two or three years, the untreated victim passes into the third and last stage of syphilis. This is the most dangerous stage. The spirochetes eat into the various body tissues and organs. They damage the nerves and destroy brain cells. Generally, late syphilis is latent, that is, no symptoms of it appear. Sometimes, though, symptoms do emerge, usually in the heart, the lungs, and the nervous system. This last stage of syphilis can continue to damage its victim for years. Sometimes it lasts for thirty years, if the victim lives that long.

We have been noting the symptoms of syphilis as they appear in various stages of the disease. We have also considered the damage inflicted on the victim of the disease during its three stages. We have not observed in detail, however, the damage which a victim can inflict on other people during the various stages. We need to see when a victim can infect other people with his disease. In the initial incubation period of the disease, in which the spirochetes multiply, but produce no symptoms, the infected person can't pass the disease on to anyone else. As soon as the sign of the first phase, the chancre, emerges, the diseased person becomes infectious. As he moves into the second phase, he develops rashes and sores loaded with spirochetes, which are highly infectious. The second phase is the period in which a person is most infectious. As long as any rash or sore lasts on a person's body, he can pass on the disease. Usually, these last for two years, and so he is infectious for two years. Although syphilis victims in the latent forms of the third stage do not pass their disease on to other adults, mothers in this stage can infect their babies with the disease through their blood, even if no sores are on the mother's body.

When anyone spots a chancre on his genitals or in his mouth, and suspects syphilis, what should he do? He should go to his private doctor or to a public health center as quickly as possible, and ask for a test for syphilis. He shouldn't ask merely for a general physical examination. This doesn't usually include a test for syphilis. The test for syphilis is a simple Davies-Hinton blood test. Usually, if a person has the disease, the blood test shows "positive" the very first time. Sometimes, however, the test doesn't show positive for as long as three months. In order to make certain that his patient doesn't have syphilis, the careful doctor usually asks him to return in another month or so for a second test. By this time, the patient should have passed into the second phase of syphilis, and then the blood test is sure to be accurate. If a patient waits too long to see a doctor and the syphilis passes into its third stage, the disease may again be difficult to diagnose accurately with a simple blood test.

If the doctor diagnoses an illness as syphilis, he begins treatment immediately. If begun early enough, treatment for syphilis, like a doctor's treatment for gonorrhea, is rapid, easy, and effective. As with gonorrhea, the doctor usually chooses penicillin in his treatment of syphilis. But, syphilis requires larger and more liberal doses of penicillin. Usually, ten doses are given, either daily or every other day. If the syphilitic patient is sensitive or immune to penicillin, a doctor may treat him with other drugs, usually antibiotics, just as he will if a patient with gonorrhea is sensitive or immune to penicillin. Experiments on the best methods of using antibiotics to cure venereal disease are currently underway. In any case, no matter who you are and no matter how you react to various drugs, you can be confident a doctor can cure your venereal disease quickly and comfortably if you see him in time.

Is there any way you can make sure you won't get syphilis? Are there any things you can take to protect yourself from the disease? No. No shot or pill has yet been developed for syphilis which immunizes you from the disease. Syphilis, too, is not like polio, or typhoid, or tetanus, from which shots do protect you. Nor does one experience with syphilis immunize you against a second or third one later, just as one experience with gonorrhea does not immunize you against another one later.

We hope you now fully understand the causes and cures for both syphilis and gonorrhea. You've seen the various symptoms of the two major strains of venereal disease. You know the signs of infection. And, at your very first suspicion of the infection, we hope you now realize you must see a doctor immediately to request diagnosis and treatment. Without this action there are always tragic effects to a person's health and to the health of people intimate with him or her. We don't take chances with venereal disease.

PART VI: MARTHA, MIKE AND MANY MORE

Having said this much, we're still not sure if you understand many of the emotional complications of VD. Many personal tragedies occur between the cause of the disease and its cure. Through knowing the seriousness of these tragedies, we can grasp the full meaning of the venereal disease problem. We think the example of Martha and Mike will communicate the depth of the disaster venereal disease can be.

Martha was a high school senior in Chicago, Illinois, who enjoyed her school and her life there. High on her list of favorite activities was dating. She was lucky because she had plenty of dates. She was a good-looking and popular girl. Imagine her as beautiful as you can. She was. Attractive as she was, she was bright as well. She was a consistent honors student with college plans. She was also gentle and generous to a fault, as we'll soon see.

Although Martha enjoyed many dates with many popular boys in her class, she'd never been asked out by *the* most intelligent, *the* most popular: Rick. Rick ranked fifth academically among the one hundred students in his class. He was vice president of the student council and captain of the football team. Girls were eager to date him, and at one time or another, he had dated most of them. But, many girls didn't seem to want to date him again, although they rarely said why. Many of the girls he dated frequently were not attractive in any way. And even some of these girls seemed relieved when they stopped dating him.

If some girls did notice the odd pattern in Rick's dating, Martha wasn't one of them. She looked up to Rick and his achievements and wondered why he'd never asked her for a date. You can imagine how she felt when Rick called her one night and asked her to go with him to the Thanksgiving football game, the most important social event of the fall. Very happy, Martha accepted.

When the big day finally came, it was perfect. Since Rick was playing halfback he couldn't pick her up at her house, but when he saw Martha in the stands he winked at her. The game began, and Martha cheered herself hoarse, but Rick's team lost by one touchdown. After the game, Rick and Martha went to a party given by one of their friends. Coke and beer were plentiful but so were some other not-so-soft items: bourbon, vodka, and marijuana. Martha didn't usually drink, but when Rick mixed one for her, she accepted it. "After all," she thought, "I do feel a little nervous. This should relax me. And I want to please Rick." She smiled. "Tastes terrific."

Soon, Rick had switched to pot. Plenty of kids at the party were trying it. After Rick took a few drags from one joint he handed it to Martha. She too took a few drags. Rick smiled and she smiled back. "He's going to be mine," she thought.

After a few more drags, Martha wasn't only relaxed, she was feeling sexually excited too. Martha never went "all the way," but she'd made out in the car and in the living room after her parents went to bed. So, Martha wasn't frightened by her excitement. Rick was obviously very excited too. He sat Martha down on a couch and wrapped his arms around her.

Martha was excited and high, too excited and too high to think much when Rick led her to an upstairs bedroom. When Rick began to caress her, she reacted by telling him, firmly (she thought), that she wouldn't make love with him. But, Rick told her how much he loved her and how much he wanted her to love him. Time and resistance slipped away and they left the bedroom an hour later.

Downstairs again, Martha was upset and embarrassed; she didn't want anyone to know what had happened to her. No longer high, she began to realize that Rick couldn't possibly love her; he'd only dated her once. She began to feel very awkward and wanted to go home. As soon as it seemed late enough, she asked Rick to drive her home. They were very quiet during the drive. When Rick was about to say goodnight, he began to apologize. "I'm really sorry, Martha," he said. "I know you're a nice girl, and I usually date not so nice girls, so I won't feel so guilty after I sleep with them. I just seem to need sex very much. I can't stop myself. Every new girl is some kind of challenge to me. Will you see me again?"

"Rick, I guess you're O.K. But, I don't want any part of this kind of thing. I want a good life. I don't want this. I don't want you. We were stupid, but O.K. . . . O.K. . . . I'm a big girl now. It happens. It . . ."

"You're going to do all right. But let me know if you change your mind."

She didn't change her mind. She worried for a month about pregnancy. Her period was a day late and she breathed a sigh of relief. But, there was a slightly heavier

This special baseball booklet, "Facts," is prepared by the Communications Materials Center of Columbia University Press to aid in the fight against venereal disease. It combines pertinent data about baseball with some hard facts about VD. If the disease is to be controlled more such public information is needed.

discharge from her vagina than she was accustomed to. She ignored it. She felt no pain.

In a few weeks, she went back to dating. She studied hard. She took a part in the class play. "I'm really doing my thing; I'm having fun, I'm learning a lot and doing social things too." Then, she met Mike.

From the beginning, she played it very carefully, even though she thought he was great. Not only did she play it carefully, she played it straight. On New Year's Eve, Mike asked her to get engaged, and she accepted. They planned the wedding for Easter vacation.

Before two people marry, they have to take tests for venereal disease. Usually only a blood test for syphilis is given but Martha and Mike lived in a state where both the blood test and the smear and culture tests for gonorrhea were given. At the time of the tests, Martha also asked for a complete physical examination, because she'd had some pain in her sex organs. She couldn't figure out what the matter was; and she wanted to be okay by the time she married Mike!

When she came to the Health Center one morning early in February, she felt more pain than ever before. When the gynecologist invited her in, she reported her pains to him and asked him what he thought the trouble might be. He examined her briefly, and then replied, "Martha, I'm afraid we have a very good idea what your problem is. Your culture test for gonorrhea was positive. From the culture, it seemed to us that you may have had this infection for a considerable period of time. If so, the chances are very good that the pain you're experiencing now comes from your fallopian tubes."

He pointed to a wall chart showing the fallopian tubes, which are located above the vagina and the uterus in the female. "The fallopian tubes are where the eggs of the female are fertilized by the sperm of the male. In these tubes, babies are conceived."

"What does all this mean?" asked Martha.

"Before I answer, I need to ask one question of you. Your reply won't go out of this room. Please be sure it's accurate. Have you made love to your fiance yet?"

"Yes, I have," Martha answered. "We really are engaged and we really will be married, so I didn't feel it was wrong. And I used EMKO, a new contraceptive foam."

"Well, EMKO isn't a very effective contraceptive. But I'm afraid pregnancy is only a part of your real problem, Martha."

"Oh?"

"Your long-term gonorrhea infection and your current pain in your fallopian tubes confirm the results of my examination here right now. You have tubal pregnancy, Martha."

"What's that?"

"One of your eggs has been fertilized in a fallopian tube by sperm. Usually, this egg would pass down into your uterus to grow into a baby. But, your fertilized egg couldn't pass down your fallopian tube to your uterus."

"Why not?" asked Martha, trying hard to understand her condition.

"Your fallopian tubes have been severely narrowed by scar tissue caused by gonorrhea. The scar tissue has almost closed your tubes. Enough space exists for sperm to travel up, but not enough space exists for a fertilized egg to travel down. Your fertilized egg is trapped. As it grows larger, it will force the walls of the tubes to expand. As the walls expand, they grow thinner and thinner; eventually they may burst. This whole condition is a very painful one, as you now know."

"Can it be cured?" asked Martha, pale with fear.

"Yes, you're lucky. You can come back tomorrow. We'll have to clean your fallopian tubes. This isn't pleasant, but it'll relieve your pain and end the danger of your tubes bursting. And, some shots of penicillin will take care of your gonorrhea. But, there's one thing we can't treat, Martha. We've gotten to your gonorrhea too late. It's done permanent damage to your fallopian tubes. We think you're sterile, Martha. You can never have a baby. I'm sorry."

Martha seemed to shrivel up in shock. She tried not to cry. She thanked the doctor and told him that she'd return the next day. Then, she hurried back to the privacy of her room as fast as she could. There, she burst into tears. "I can never have a baby. I wanted a family so much. What will Mike think? I'll have to tell him why I'm sterile. Then he'll know that I wasn't a virgin when we met." Each thought seemed more terrible than the last.

That evening, Martha called up Mike and said they'd better meet for a date, not in his room with his other roommates as they'd planned, but in a place they could be alone. Mike suggested the Casa 8, a small coffee house. As soon as Mike met Martha there, he realized something was very wrong.

"Martha, what happened?"

"I was at the Health Center today. Remember the pain

I've been having in my stomach? The doctors have diagnosed it. I've got a tubal pregnancy."

"What's that?"

"It's a bad kind of pregnancy you get when your fallopian tubes are blocked up. Mine are blocked up from gonorrhea."

"Oh, Martha, please . . . no. I've never been to bed with anyone but you. There's nothing wrong with me. If there was, I'd have known it by now."

"Mike, I'm sorry. I should have told you this a long time ago. Earlier this year, I got high at a party and slept with this guy. It doesn't even make any difference who he is, now. But I heard later he slept around a lot; anybody, just anybody. He must have had it. I remember now, I had a heavy discharge quite a long time after that night with him, but I've always had some discharge, and I never thought anything of it."

Mike looked very upset. "Martha, this is awful. I thought you were a virgin; you always seemed so innocent. But don't worry; I love you. I can forgive you. Maybe not tonight, and maybe not tomorrow, but I'll forgive you."

"Mike, there's still something I have to tell you. The doctor told me about something else besides my tubal pregnancy. He said I'm sterile. We can never have a baby." Martha cried on Mike's shoulder.

Mike could say nothing. To himself, he thought, "I've always dreamed of a family, not a big family, but maybe two kids, a boy and a girl. I want to do well in the world; but what will success mean without a family to share it? Can I really marry Martha when I know we can never have kids to share our happiness and be part of our love?"

                                    VENEREAL DISEASE

The couple spent almost three hours at the Casa 8. On and off, Martha wept and Mike tried to comfort her. It just didn't work. Maybe, just maybe, he didn't really mean it. When he left Martha that night, he promised he'd call her the next day, but he didn't. Instead, he sent her a note which read:

"Dear Martha:

I love you, I think I forgive you. But I know I want a family and I know that I can't stand the idea of our not being able to have one. I'd make you miserable, I'd make myself miserable. I'm sorry, Martha, but I'm breaking our engagement."

Martha cried again. She wished that she had never loved anybody. She wished that she could start from where she had been, before all this had happened. "If only . . . if only . . .," she said, and she'd repeat the words many times in her life, but never be able to make them sound any better.

PART VII: FOUR THOUSAND NEW YORKERS

Martha and Mike's story illustrates well, we think, the personal difficulties which often result from venereal disease. Other tragic consequences result from the disease, too, in a more social sense. The disease can hurt not only one or two people, but many people. Perhaps the story of some forty New Yorkers, who began a venereal disease epidemic which led to infection of more than four thousand people, will show you the social consequences of venereal disease, as well as the story of Mike and Martha did the personal consequences. The story is told by the New York City Venereal Disease Clinic, which tried to stop the epidemic but failed. In the process, the clinic assembled and analyzed the cases which began the epidemic. For each patient, this and other clinics keep all information confidential and not for prosecution.

When Betty went to her doctor because of a bad cold she couldn't shake, she furnished the first clue to the epidemic in the lower East Side of New York City. The doctor made a routine Hinton blood test. The test was positive and the doctor diangosed Betty's "cold" as syphillis in its secondary stage. The doctor sent Betty to the City Venereal Disease Clinic, which treated her and tried to discover her other sexual contacts.

Betty, a twenty-five-year-old woman, was married to a man who drank heavily and who often beat her when he was drunk. But, although Betty had left her husband, Frank, several times after he'd beaten her, she'd never had an affair with another man, and named Frank as her only sexual contact.

When Betty told Frank she had visited the clinic, he became angry with her, got drunk and was arrested for disorderly conduct. Having talked to a policeman about his wife's VD while intoxicated, Frank was brought by one man on the force to the clinic the next morning. To the nurse, Frank admitted that he had sores on his penis some months ago. The nurse's suspicion of syphilis was supported by the results of a blood test. When pushed to give the names of his sexual contacts, Frank confessed that in the last six months he had experienced relations not only with his wife, but also with Kathy, whom he described as a "nice girl, a good-looking girl, but almost a whore."

Divorced at nineteen, Kathy was very much as Frank thought her to be. When she reached twenty-one, she had had three children, two of whom were illegitimate. Kathy was a favorite girl of many men in the area. She never turned anyone away. Sometimes, she'd take money for her services; sometimes she wouldn't. Her attitude towards money seemed to depend on her attitude toward her sexual partner. Her favorite sexual partners never paid.

When Kathy was contacted and brought into the clinic and was found to be infected with syphilis, she named six men with whom she had had sex. These six men might have escaped paying Kathy for her services, but they didn't escape VD. The clinic contacted them and found them all infected. As the clinic treated these men, they tried to figure out the names of the people whom they had contacted recently to treat them and thus curb the epidemic.

Jules was a thirty-year-old man who had deserted his wife, "because she was frigid." Although he claimed to have been in love with a "warm, beautiful girl," Phyllis, for several months, his feeling for her didn't keep him any closer to her than it had to his wife. He had enjoyed Kathy several times during these months. Now, he had several sores on his penis from his experiences. Jules' description of Phyllis as "warm" seemed only too true. Only fifteen years old, Phyllis confessed to sexual relations with four other men, all over twenty-five. Two of the four were diagnosed as having syphilis.

Next, the clinic contacted Larry, a twenty-four year old married man who imagined himself an Adonis, particularly when he was high on drugs. In these intoxicated conditions he almost always visited Kathy, who seemed the one girl who flattered him as much as he liked. In spite of his need to seem godlike, however, Larry was very cooperative at the clinic. He named the three other girls he had had relations with in the last six months and helped to bring them and some of Kathy's other contacts into the clinic. Oddly enough, his sexual contacts did not include his wife.

One of the men Larry led to the clinic was Robert. Robert, twenty-six years old, was the father of one of Kathy's illegitimate children. By all accounts, Robert had shown very little interest in the year-old child. Perhaps one of the reasons he had decided not to stay with Kathy and his child was his homosexual tendency. Although he didn't confess to having sexual contact, he confessed to sleeping in the same bed with one boy, Sam. When Sam was brought in for diagnosis, he was found to be infected with syphilis. Sam was only fourteen years old. He reported no other physical contacts.

A few days later, the clinic saw George, a twenty-six-year-old single man who lived with his younger sister. George was active in sports, but not on the job. He worked once in a while, but usually let his sister feed him, buy him clothes, and generally support him. When he was called to the clinic because Kathy had named him as a contact, he was found to have both syphilis and gonorrhea. Apparently, he'd gotten gonorrhea from one of his other sexual partners. These partners seemed numerous. George propositioned almost every girl friend his sister had. Of the five girls George named, three were contacted. One, Lorraine, had gonorrhea. She confessed to several other sexual contacts. They were also summoned to the clinic, but not all responded to the summons. As a result, many of George's friends weren't treated and continued to spread the epidemic.

Carl and Zack were two brothers involved with Kathy. Kathy claimed they'd both met her in a bar, and started to fight for the privilege of taking her home, when Kathy "straightened out" the situation by inviting them both back to her room for "some kicks." She kept the pair under control for a while, but after sexual relations with Kathy, the two fought again. Kathy was glad when they decided to fight it out on the street. It took a month until the brothers found they'd received syphilis as well as black eyes.

When Zack and Carl came to the clinic, only Carl reported other sexual contacts. Zack seemed too embarrassed. Of the three girls Carl named, one, Beatrice, provided the clinic with a distressing but important clue to why the epidemic was not under control despite the clinic's efforts. She named David as one of her sexual partners. David, it turned out, was Kathy's eighteen-year-old brother. Young as he was, David was married. He seemed sullen and angry and the clinic was not surprised by his report that his wife had recently left him, with the result that he'd been "playing around." He named several contacts in his first interview at the clinic. During his second, he told the nurse abruptly that he'd decided to admit another contact. He named his sister, Kathy.

From David's report of his sister's sexual behavior, the clinic realized that Kathy was a good deal more promiscuous than she had confessed. Putting David's report together with several other men's, the clinic judged that Kathy probably had shared sex with triple the number of men she had named. The clinic concluded further that Kathy was a major source of the syphilis outbreak in the lower East Side of the city, an outbreak soon to involve over four thousand people. This was largely because the clinic hadn't been able to contact and treat all of Kathy's sexual partners. Only if the clinic had been able to persuade Kathy to confess her other sexual contacts, could the epidemic have been quickly arrested. And, only when the clinic curbed the epidemic, could it have been assured that people wouldn't suffer serious damage from syphilis.

The clinic's analysis of the infected people it treated may interest you. The clinic found the average age of female patients about nineteen, and the average age of male patients about twenty-two. Generally, the patients were

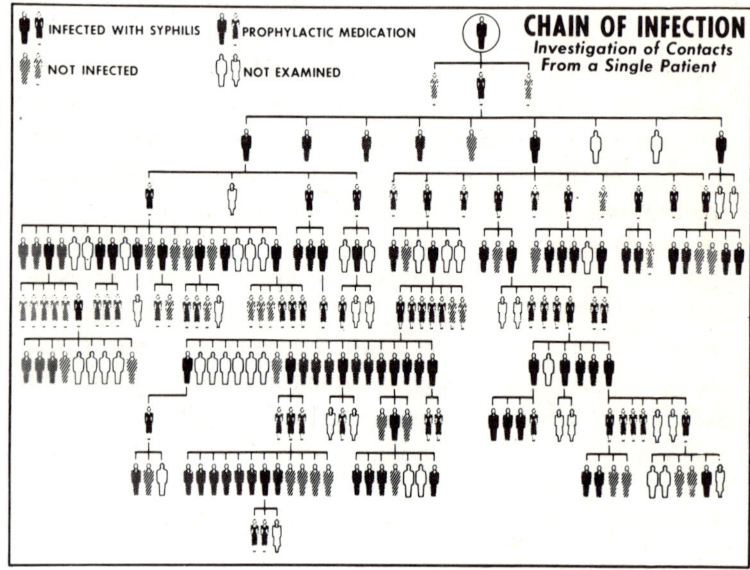

This astonishing chart shows how a syphilis epidemic can spread from one original infected person. Kathy was a good example. The outbreak that she was largely responsible for starting ultimately involved over four thousand people.

not poor. Most had some skills, held jobs and lived in decent areas. All but two of the patients were white.

From these facts, we may conclude that these infected people were Americans with average social and economic standings. Whatever the social and economic standings of these people, however, they were at no less risk of infection. They were usually unrestrained sexually and seemed to show no concern, much less guilt, over their behavior. They often held so little affection, sympathy or concern for the welfare of their sexual partners that they wouldn't reveal their names and thus enable them to be contacted and helped by the clinic.

From our report on the New York epidemic, we should now realize how the pattern of lack of sexual restraint contributes to the spread of these epidemics. Such attitudes must be changed if VD outbreaks are to be stopped. In our next chapter, we'll probe this and other avenues of attack against VD.

PART VIII: HOW CAN VD BE PREVENTED?

The methods of preventing VD are many and varied. Perhaps the two basic types of methods are first, those which treat victims in an effort to prevent their spreading the disease; and second, those which treat non-victims in an effort to prevent their catching the disease. The efforts of Public Health Clinics fall largely into the first category. Legal efforts and educational efforts fall into both. Squarely in the second category is the effort to establish guidelines for development of attitudes, which we concluded to be crucial in our last chapter. Only if all these efforts are carried out to their fullest will the growth of VD be checked.

In our account of a syphilis epidemic in New York City, we noted great effort by the Venereal Disease Clinic to arrest the spread of the epidemic. We observed their practices not only for the treatment of victims of the disease but also in questioning the victims for the names of their recent sexual partners in an attempt to contact and treat these people, too. This attempt to track down as many exposed people as possible is basic to controlling VD. In health terminology, this attempt is called epidemiology.

Venereal disease epidemiology is an advanced science. Venereal disease clinics know exactly how to interview patients in order to gain from them exact identification of

Tracking down syphilis "contacts" is a difficult problem. Above, a worker for the U.S. Public Health Service checks his book on a New York street. He is one of a group of devoted men who work overtime tracking down spreaders of venereal disease, again on the increase in the U.S. The black bag holds equipment for blood tests.

their sexual contacts, who are also possible VD victims. The truly professional nurse who interviews the patients tries not to embarrass them. She doesn't read them a page on morality, for she knows they may not return to the clinic if she does. She indicates to them that the names of their sexual contacts will be kept strictly confidential. Then, she begins the interview. She asks for the name of all sexual contacts; the full name and the nickname, if the contact has one. Few interviewers accept the statement, "I don't know the person's name," for rarely does someone approach a stranger and immediately propose an intimate relationship.

Second on the interview agenda is the request for the address of all sexual contacts. If the patient can't remember the exact address of the contact, the interviewer asks him to describe in as much detail as possible the particular dwelling. Next, the patient is asked to describe each contact personally. The age, sex, color, face, figure, and style of dress of the contact are all vital pieces of information. "What does your contact do?" is usually the next question. Hopefully, the answer includes the marital status, occupation, hours of work, and after-work types and places of recreation.

Then, the patient is requested to discuss his relationship with the contact and the date, place, and manner of their meeting at the time of VD exposure. Knowledge of the particular strain of VD to which the contact was exposed is also gained. If any data suggest the contact is pregnant, she is traced with particular speed and care. She's rated "an epidemiological emergency." Generally, if the patient answers all the questions honestly and fully, the chances that a nurse can track the contact down are good. If a patient fails to answer questions well, the nurse usually asks him to return, not only once but often twice, to fill informational gaps and give the nurse a better chance of tracing the contact.

You may be interested in learning more about these venereal disease clinics which help so much to stop epidemics. Usually, the VD clinic is a division of a Public Health Clinic. The average clinic serves patients in the working and welfare classes, mostly between fifteen and twenty-five years old. Many patients don't know what venereal disease is. Often they don't even know how to pronounce the names of the diseases. Many are anxious and embarrassed about their infection, but many others are unemotional about it and return frequently to the clinic with the same disease.

The clinics themselves serve patients without charge. They're supported by the state. They usually receive about $3,000 a month from the state's Department of Public Health. Clinics are located in almost every large town in the United States. Whereas clinics are run by the states, one agency, the Division of Communicable Diseases, is supported by the federal government and gives services to the state clinics.

The Division of Communicable Diseases makes the laboratory tests, studies VD trends, and keeps the states up to date on these trends. It also helps to educate the people by distributing films and pamphlets. Recently, the Division has also been trying to develop a shot to treat a Vietnamese strain of venereal disease which isn't easily cured by penicillin. There are many different strains of VD. We talk

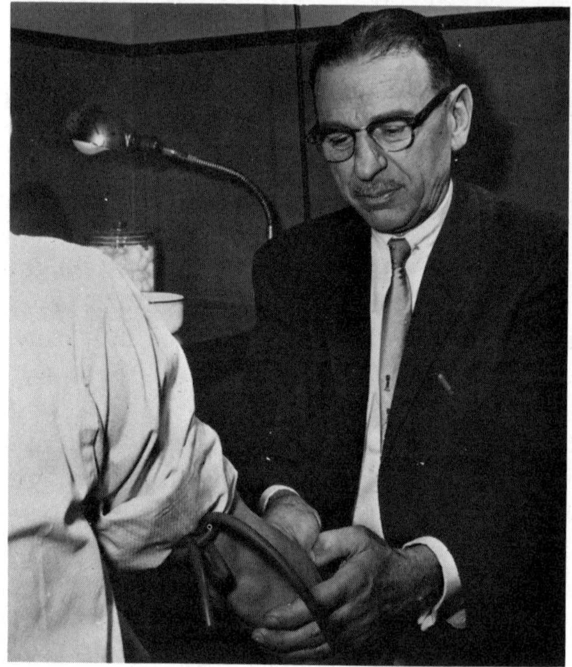

A doctor, who is chief of a hygiene clinic in the Chelsea section of New York City, tests a man who has been exposed to syphilis. City, federal and international health agents cooperate in tracing contacts who may be spreading the disease.

just of gonorrhea and syphilis primarily because they are
the only two significant strains prevalent in the United
States.

Now that we've taken a look at state and federal agencies
and the methods which they use to curb VD, let's look at a
second method for preventing the disease. This method is
the law. The law backs up the epidemiological efforts of the
health clinics by requiring that private doctors report cases
to the clinics. The law also tries to catch VD victims and to
prevent people from becoming victims. In an effort to
catch VD victims, the law demands that people be tested
at various times in their lives for VD. The Selective Service
checks its young men in a physical exam. States require
physicians to test pregnant women for syphilis and to treat
them for it if they have it. States also demand that persons
be checked for syphilis before they secure a marriage
license. And we've already noticed that by law all babies
receive eye drops at birth to prevent blindness from
gonorrhea infection.

Other laws try to stop VD before it starts. They attack
immoral practices. Most states outlaw prostitution, forni-
cation, and adultery. Generally, these laws don't seem as
effective in preventing these practices as laws requiring
tests for VD are in catching the victims of the practices.

A third weapon in the arsenal used against VD is
education. Educational campaigns aim first at VD victims.
They try to alert victims to the symptoms of their
infections and warn them of the importance of seeing a
doctor immediately. In this way the hope of preventing
permanent damage to the victim and of curbing any
chances of a VD epidemic is realized. A second target of

educational campaigns is the potential VD victim. The campaign tries to warn these potential victims against contact with promiscuous people who are likely to have VD. It tries to set up guidelines for attitudes concerned with sexual contact.

What kind of moral codes would help our people steer clear of VD? It's very difficult to set up a strict, rigid code which will work for everyone. But, it isn't so difficult to indicate what kinds of behavior will almost inevitably bring trouble, both physically and mentally. One example of such behavior is the destructive conduct of the New Yorkers who began the syphilis epidemic. Another example is Margie's behavior.

Margie was only thirteen years old when she started having sexual relations with men. She'd been brought up in a comfortable family; poverty wasn't her problem. Rather, her difficulty seemed to be a lack of attention at home. Her father spent long hours working and her mother, burdened with six children, spent all her time cooking, washing, and cleaning the house. All her children had sought attention and affection outside their home as soon as they could.

For two years, Margie continued to have affairs without becoming pregnant. Although the affairs rarely seemed to last, probably because most boys resented her possessive nature, she seemed to find some satisfaction in them. She was never told by her family that her behavior was wrong and that, in the long run, she would suffer because she had cheapened sex. She never seemed to find in sex the real love which can be part of it.

Then, two years after her first sexual experience, Margie

was infected with gonorrhea. She discovered her illness when she was called to a clinic after an infected boy friend named her as a sexual contact. She didn't tell her mother because "Mom has enough problems of her own." She felt she might get upset, but really wouldn't care. Then, the doctors found her gonorrhea difficult to treat and sent her to an emergency ward for special care. The doctor called Margie's mother and told her of her daughter's problem, but the mother showed no concern. She bought birth control pills for her, but gave her none of the understanding or moral advice which would help her live a better life.

The doctor cured Margie's gonorrhea that time. Now twenty, Margie returns to the clinic almost once a year with a new case of gonorrhea. She is a sad girl. She knows no one loves her, although many sleep with her. She needs love badly but doesn't realize she could have found it only if she waited until she became more emotionally mature. Only then could she have a reasonable chance for a truly loving relationship.

From these accounts, you probably see what we mean by responsible sexual conduct. We mean that responsible conduct involves a sense of social as well as personal responsibilities. We mean that if you don't find yourself able to confine physical intimacy to one person, you must at least then assume social responsibility for your sexual practices. To be more blunt, we mean that if you contract venereal disease, you must accept the responsibility of going to a doctor, getting it treated, and reporting the names of your other sexual contacts.

We believe sex is often destructive and meaningless unless it's shared by two people in love. And we mean that mature love can only exist between two people who *are* mature, who have really worked to achieve a relationship. It can only exist between two people who try to understand each other's needs and attitudes, and who feel and act responsibly toward each other.

PART IX: VD: FACTS AND FALLACIES

Because persons, young or old, would like to know more about what they observe to be part of the venereal disease picture, it is very important that we talk about many things "known," which are wholly or partially untrue. We are talking about a number of untruths which seem to be commonly believed and which have lasted a surprisingly long time even though scientists have made great strides. Sometimes, these untruths seem, by their very nature, to be more resistant to change than the facts. We offer the following fallacies and facts concerning VD, in order to make open and clear what is true and what is not. In addition, we have also included some popular "myths" about sex in general.

FALLACY	FACT
Wet dreams mean loss of manhood or of strength.	Wet dreams are natural during maturation and have no weakening effect.
If the penis or testicles are small in size, a male is less virile.	There is no evidence that the size of the sex organs affects masculinity.
Men who are hairy are more manly.	There is no evidence to support this statement.
It is unwise for girls to bathe or to shampoo during their menstrual periods.	Cleanliness during the menstrual period is particularly important both because of the menstrual flow and the fact that many girls perspire more freely at that time.
The menstrual period lasts from three to four days.	Variations from two to eight days are considered normal.
The absence of the hymen in a girl is evidence that she is not a virgin.	Neither the presence nor the absence of the hymen is considered a criterion of virginity.
When a girl is menstruating, she is sick.	Menstrual flow has nothing to do with illness.

Girls can expect to experience abdominal pain during their monthly periods.

Menstrual cramps are psychological unless there is actual organic disturbance.

Nocturnal emissions occur because a boy has bad thoughts.

Nocturnal emissions are physiological phenomena which do not always result from psychological processes.

The size of a girl's breasts and the size of a boy's penis determine their femininity and masculinity.

Only when physical organs produce negative feelings about one's sexual adequacy are they important.

Boys and girls who have had inadequate or negative sex instruction will be forever handicapped in achieving psychosexual maturity.

With sincere effort and proper instruction, plus professional help, individuals can overcome negative attitudes and reach a healthy maturity.

A girl can become pregnant from kissing.

Kissing never produces pregnancy.

Since boys are more easily aroused sexually than girls are, the responsibility for moral behavior is the girl's.

Both boys and girls should assume responsibility for their sexual behavior.

Homosexuality can be detected by an individual's appearance.

It is unjust and foolhardy to label an individual homosexual because of his appearance.

Homosexuality can never be cured.

With sincere effort and desire to change, plus professional help, homosexuals can often overcome this psychosexual handicap.

Adolescents can expect their teen years to be painful and traumatic.

Not all adolescents experience difficulty in making the transition to maturity.

Steady dating at an early age must be a good idea because so many young people do it.

Steady dating at too early an age can be harmful to psychosexual and psychosocial development.

French or soul kissing is unnatural.

Passionate kissing is natural, but it is so sexually stimulating it can easily lead to more serious sexual behavior.

Masturbation causes sterility.

There is no connection between masturbation and sterility.

Masturbation causes insanity.

The act of masturbation does not cause insanity; however, the feelings of guilt and shame can lead to personality maladjustment.

Sexual compatibility is the best basis for a happy marriage.

Psychological compatibility is more important than sexual compatibility for a happy marriage.

Impotence and frigidity are usually organic in origin.

Impotence and frigidity are more frequently psychologically determined.

A truly feminine woman relates well only to men.

A truly feminine woman relates well to both sexes.

A boy who has no father or a physically inadequate father will never become a real man.

Though a boy who has a strong masculine father probably has less difficulty in becoming masculine himself, other strong male figures such as teachers or brothers or uncles can provide the necessary identification model.

Girls who parade their femininity have a stronger sex identity.

Extreme emphasis on sex by dress or manner frequently is indicative of an uncertain sex identity.

The "sexual revolution" is an unhealthy social development.	The "sexual revolution" is a social phenomenon which reflects changing ideas regarding sex and sex behavior.
Excessive bleeding during menstruation is good because it cleanses the body of impurities.	Menstrual flow has no relation to impurity.
No sexual play, interest, or activity can take place before puberty.	Sexual play and interest may occur even before the latency period.
All sexual inhibitions and problems disappear at marriage.	Marriage can intensify sexual problems.
Self-diagnosis of VD is relatively simple since symptoms are obvious.	Only a doctor can tell if you have VD.
VD can be caught from a toilet seat or a doorknob.	VD is contracted through personal contact.
Syphilis is not likely to become more serious than a skin rash.	Syphilis can cause heart disease, insanity, paralysis, blindness, deafness, and a number of deformities.

A gonorrhea infection in women is easily spotted.

Women may have the disease without symptoms.

Immunity to VD can be developed after a number of exposures and cures.

There is no such acquired immunity to VD.

Drug store aids (condoms and salves) provide certain protection from VD.

No drug store aid can provide 100% protection against VD infection.

It is expensive and risky to your reputation to seek medical treatment for VD.

Many local health departments have free diagnosis and treatment clinics where patients receive confidential care.

The risk of death from VD is far less than from diseases like small-pox and polio.

Every year more people die from syphilis than from both of these two diseases, plus typhoid and plague.

There are some pills which can prevent syphilis if taken before sexual intercourse.

There are no drugs known which can prevent infection in this way.

Urination can cause most of the germs to be flushed out so that infection is prevented.

Urination cannot measurably affect the risk of infection.

Gonorrhea or "clap" isn't
really much more serious
than a kind of cold in the
sexual organs.

This disease which frequently
causes pus to be discharged
from the sexual organs can result in blindness, arthritis,
and sterility.

Finding and using a salve
containing penicillin is almost a sure way of knocking
out the disease
of syphilis.

Usually penicillin salve will
kill off the top layers of the
disease and only disguise the
symptoms; medical aid is es-
sential for cure.

Treatment for both syphilis
and gonorrhea by a physician
is both very long and painful.

The use of current medical knowledge and drugs makes treatment
both short-term and nearly pain-
less if the cure is begun at an
early stage of the disease by a
licensed physician.

Naming sexual contacts to
public health officials
can be very incriminating
for them and for you.

All health department venereal
disease records are strictly
confidential and are used for
treatment and prevention, not
prosecution.

"Venereal disease" means just that and the infection is always confined to the venery or sexual organ.

Sores (particularly from syphilis) may appear in many locations on the body; thus some VD may be transmitted by kissing an area that may look like a cold sore.

Over the last six years, the VD problem has stayed about the same.

In that period, yearly infections of syphilis have tripled. Cities report VD rates up 800 percent and we are moving towards a figure of two million new cases a year.

If you're lucky enough to have the early rash of syphilis disappear without treatment, you've beaten the disease.

Early symptoms almost always disappear, leaving the body, in fact, more dangerously diseased than before.

If you passed the test for syphilis, you can also assume that you don't have gonorrhea.

The two tests for the diseases are completely independent and one method cannot be used as a substitute for the other.

Most of the victims of VD are over 26 and really ought to know better.

Most of the victims of VD are under 25, one out of five is a teenager, and *they* really ought to have known better.

PART X: GLOSSARY

Adolescence - The period of development between child-
hood and adulthood, beginning with puberty and marked
by gradual and continuous maturation of organic, psychological and social factors in personality.

Adrenal Glands - A pair of endocrine or ductless glands,
located over the kidneys, which have an important relation
to emotional responses.

Ambivalence - Simultaneous feelings of attraction to and
repulsion from some person or object.

Compulsion - A strong and sometimes irresistible, im-
pulse to perform some act even though it is thought to be
unreasonable.

Condom - Artificial covering of the penis to assist in
preventing conception or infection.

Copulation - Sexual intercourse.

Diagnosis - A clinical process by which the nature and
classification of any disorder is determined by analysis of
symptoms.

Epidemiology - The branch of medicine that deals with epidemics.

Erotic - Of or pertaining to sex or sexual love.

Frigidity (sexual) - Reduction or absence of sexual desire, usually caused by emotional disturbance.

Gonads - The primary organs of the reproductive systems of the male (the testes) and the female (the ovaries).

Gonococcus - The germ which transmits gonorrhea.

Gonorrhea - A contagious, pus-containing inflammation of the urethra or the vagina, caused by invasion of the gonococcus.

Guilt, Sense of - The feeling or conviction of having violated some principle, rule, or law.

Heterosexual - Pertaining to the other sex, or to relations between the sexes.

Homosexual - Sexual desire for, or contact with, members of the same sex.

Hormone - A specific chemical substance secreted by an endocrine gland that induces changes in the activities of other organs.

Hymen - Thin membrane partially closing the opening of the vagina.

Impotence - Inability of the male to perform the sexual act.

Lesbianism - Homosexuality in the female.

Masturbation - Manual stimulation of any genital organ or orgasm.

Maturation - The process whereby organisms, processes, or functions reach a stage of complete growth or development. The state of full development is called maturity.

Menstruation - Periodic discharge from non-pregnant, breeding-age women of blood and tissue debris from the uterus.

Morbidity - The condition of being diseased.

Nocturnal Emissions ("wet dreams") - periodic nocturnal release of seminal fluid in the developing adolescent male occurring when the testes have produced an excess amount of fluid.

Promiscuity - Indiscriminate sexual activity, usually in terms of number of partners rather than frequency.

Psychosexual - Pertaining to sexual functions and development involving psychological processes and conditions.

Psychosocial - A term used to refer to processes or traits that are determined jointly by psychological and social conditions.

Puberty - The period of life during which the reproductive functions become operative; the beginning of sexual maturation.

Self-concept - An individual's personal idea of himself, including his attitudes, ideals, principles, values, and so on; the self-ideal.

Self-image - The way in which one sees himself in terms of his physical image, behavior, aptitudes, and values; not necessarily firmly based in reality.

Sex Characteristics - Physical changes related to sexual development:
   a (Primary—changes within the sexual system such as growth of the sex organs, nocturnal emissions, and menstruation.
   b) Secondary—changes related to sex organ activity, but outside of the sexual system such as the appearance of body hair and the activity of the axillary (armpit) sweat glands.

Syndrome - A more or less organized group of symptoms occurring together and characteristic of a certain disorder.

Syphilis - A chronic, infectious venereal disease, caused by a micro-organism, spirochaeta pallida, and communicated by sexual contact. There are three stages: primary, secondary, and tertiary, characterized by chancre formation, skin affections, and affections of bones, muscles, and nervous system.

Venereal - Arising from or connected with sexual intercourse with an infected person (venereal disease).